My

This book is dedicated to my son, Kasey, my nephews, Jaxon, Drew and Greighson, my niece, Harper, and my great-nieces, Aliyah and Alyssa.

You are the future, and I pray that you always walk in faith, confidence and courage.

May you all Pray Like Elijah!

Acknowledgments

To my father, Robert Sr. (in memory), and my mother, Dottie "Co-Author" Beard, for your endless love and wisdom. To my sister Paulette and my brother Rodney, thank you for always believing in me.

To my in-laws, Domonique and Samuel, Chris Jr. and Miya, Megan and Brennan My god-sisters, Angela "Angie", Naomi, Faye, and Renee—your support is greatly appreciated.

To my nieces, Rae'Von and Christina, my nephews, Dustin and Paul, and Cayim, you continue to inspire me.

To my Revelation Church family, you all made me fall in love with church again! Let's continue to expand the Kingdom one person at a time.

Lastly to my wife, La'Keisha, thank you for always supporting and loving me.

PRAYING LIKE ELIJAH" is a journey of faith, persistence, and the power of prayer. Inspired by the life of Elijah. This book is designed to help you grow spiritually, connect with God, and discover how powerful your prayers can be. Through stories, prayer prompts, and reflections, you'll learn how faith can move mountains and change lives.

As you walk through this journey, I hope you will be encouraged to deepen your relationship with God and understand that, like Elijah, your prayers have the potential to bring hope, healing, and transformation to the world around you.

WEEK ONE

Elijah

and the

Epic Rain

Dance

Once upon a time, in a vibrant neighborhood, in San Bernardino, California, there was a terrible drought. The streets were dusty, the trees were dry, and everyone was thirsty. But there was one thing they hadn't lost, and that's hope.

A kid named Elijah believed deep in his heart that prayer could bring them the rain they desperately needed.

Elijah had a squad of friends who trusted him because he was always coming up with incredible ideas. One scorching afternoon, Elijah stood up and said, "Hey fam, this morning, I heard Holy Spirit say that God will bring the rain if we believe and pray. Who's with me?"

His best friend, Kareem, looked up at the clear, blue sky and chuckled, "Man, there isn't a cloud in sight. But you know what, I'm with you, bro."

Elijah gathered everyone on the rooftop—a place where they could see the whole city and feel closer to the sky. With heads bowed and hands together, they began to pray. Elijah's voice flowed like a smooth hip-hop rhythm, "God, we know You hear us. We need some rain, and we trust you to make it happen. Show us Your power, because we have the faith!"

After the prayer, Elijah asked Kareem to check the sky. Kareem ran to the edge of the rooftop, scanned the horizon, and came back shaking his head, "Nothing, Elijah."

But Elijah wasn't discouraged. "It's cool, check again." He told Kareem to go back seven times, and each time Kareem came back with the same answer—no clouds. But Elijah's faith never wavered.

On the seventh trip, Kareem squinted at the horizon. "Wait a minute! I see something. It's tiny, like a little puff of smoke."

Elijah's face lit up with excitement. "That's it! God's sending us rain. Everybody get ready!"

As they waited, the sky started to change. Dark clouds rolled in, and the wind began to pick up. Suddenly, the heavens opened up, and rain began to pour down. It was like the city had come to life! People ran out of their homes, dancing and singing in the rain, their faith rewarded.

Elijah and his friends performed an epic rain dance, celebrating the miracle they had prayed for. They knew that prayer, mixed with unwavering faith, could make incredible things happen.

DAY 1

"Do not worry about anything. But pray and ask God for everything you need. And when you pray, always give thanks."

Philippians 4:6 (ICB)

Prayer Prompt

Ask God to help you feel calm when you're worried.

Activity

Draw a picture of something that makes you feel happy and peaceful.

DAY 2

"The Lord is my shepherd. I have everything I need."
Psalm 23:1 (ICB)

Prayer Prompt

Thank God for taking care of you like a shepherd takes care of sheep.

Activity

Make a list of three things you're thankful for and share it with a family member.

DAY 3

"The Spirit helps us with our weakness. We do not know how to pray as we should. But the Spirit himself speaks to God for us."
Romans 8:26 (ICB)

Prayer Prompt

Ask the Holy Spirit to help you when you don't know what to pray for.

Activity

Write down or draw something that makes you feel unsure, then pray for God to help.

DAY 4

"The thing you should want most is God's kingdom and doing what God wants."
Matthew 6:33 (ICB)

Prayer Prompt

Pray that you will always seek God first in everything you do.

Activity

Create a treasure map and mark "God" as the most important treasure.

DAY 5

"But the people who trust the Lord will become strong again. They will be able to rise up as an eagle in the sky."
Isaiah 40:31 (ICB)

Prayer Prompt

Ask God to give you strength when you feel tired.

Activity

Pretend to be an eagle and flap your wings for 30 seconds while saying, "God gives me strength!"

DAY 6

"But if any of you needs wisdom, you should ask God for it. He is generous and enjoys giving to everyone."
James 1:5 (ICB)

Prayer Prompt

Ask God for wisdom to make good choices.

Activity

Write down one decision you need to make. Ask God to help you with it.

DAY 7

"Be still and know that I am God."
Psalm 46:10 (ICB)

Prayer Prompt

Pray for quiet time to listen to God.

Activity

Sit in a quiet spot for 2 minutes and listen. Draw or write what you felt during the quiet time.

Week 2

Elijah and the Glowing Lantern

The rain had come and quenched the city's thirst, but that was just the beginning of Elijah's adventures. With faith riding high, Elijah and his friends knew they had a special mission—to spread the word about the power of prayer.

A few years later, one night, as Elijah was heading home from basketball practice, he noticed something glowing under a tree in the park. Curious, he went over and found an old, weathered lantern. The light inside was flickering like it was trying to tell him something. He picked it up and felt a warmth run through his fingers.

Just then, his friend, Leila, came jogging by. "Hey, Elijah, what's that?"

Elijah shrugged, "I don't know, but I think it's special. Maybe it's a sign."

They gathered the rest of their crew—Kareem, Tony, and Mia—and sat in a circle around the lantern. Elijah held it up and said, "We've seen what faith can do. This lantern feels like it's here for a reason. Let's pray and see what happens."

As they prayed, the light in the lantern grew brighter and brighter until it filled the whole park with a soft, golden glow. Suddenly, they heard a gentle voice, "Keep your faith strong, and this light will guide you."

The kids were amazed. Elijah said, "This light is our reminder. Every time we see it, we'll remember to pray and believe. We got to share this with everyone!"

They decided to take the lantern around their city, telling everyone their story. They visited schools, community centers, and even made a quick video that went viral on social media. People from all over started sending messages, sharing their own stories of faith and prayer.

One day, a young girl named Aisha sent them a message. She was in the hospital, battling a tough illness, but she had seen their video and started praying with all her heart. Her message read, "Your story gave me hope. I'm praying every day, and I believe God is going to help me get better."

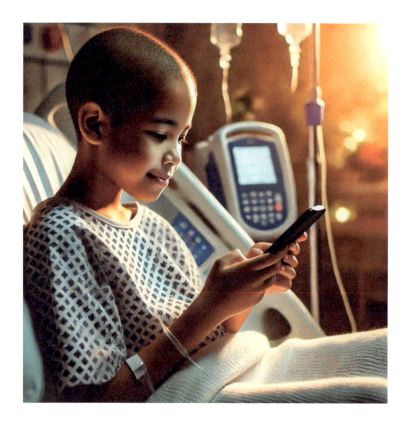

Elijah and his friends were touched. They knew they had to visit her. They brought the glowing lantern to her hospital room, and together, they prayed for her healing. The room filled with the same warm light, and everyone could feel the power of their faith.

Aisha smiled and said, "I feel stronger already. Thank you for showing me the power of prayer."

DAY 8

"Always be full of joy. Never stop praying. Give thanks whatever happens."
1 Thessalonians 5:16-18 (ICB)

Prayer Prompt

Thank God for all the good things in your life, even when things are hard.

Activity

Make a "thankful jar" and write down one thing you're thankful for each day to put inside.

DAY 9

"Trust the Lord with all your heart. Don't depend on your own understanding."
Proverbs 3:5-6 (ICB)

Prayer Prompt

Pray that you will trust God, even when you don't understand something.

Activity

Close your eyes and let someone guide you through a short walk in your house, trusting them to lead you — just like you trust God.

DAY 10

"Wear the full armor of God. Wear God's armor so that you can fight against the devil's evil tricks."
Ephesians 6:11 (ICB)

Prayer Prompt

Ask God to protect you from bad things and help you make good choices.

Activity

Draw your own "Armor of God" and label each part (helmet, shield, etc.).

DAY 11

"I am the vine, and you are the branches. If anyone remains in me and I remain in him, then he will produce much fruit. But without me he can do nothing."
John 15:5 (ICB)

Prayer Prompt

Pray to stay connected to Jesus like branches are connected to a tree.

Activity

Draw a tree and label each branch with ways you can stay close to Jesus (like prayer or reading the Bible).

DAY 12

"You are the people of God. He chose you to belong to him. So, you must clothe yourselves with compassion, kindness, humility, gentleness, and patience."
Colossians 3:12 (ICB)

Prayer Prompt

Ask God to help you be kind and patient with others.

Activity

Make a "kindness card" for someone and give it to them or leave it somewhere they'll find it.

DAY 13

"Your word is like a lamp for my feet and a light for my way."
Psalm 119:105 (ICB)

Prayer Prompt

Ask God to show you the right path to take in your life.

Activity

Draw a path on a piece of paper and write one way God can guide you on that path.

DAY 14

"But the Spirit gives love, joy, peace, patience, kindness, goodness, faithfulness, gentleness, and self-control."
Galatians 5:22-23 (ICB)

Prayer Prompt

Pray for the fruit of the Spirit, like love and joy, to grow in your heart.

Activity

Create a "Fruit of the Spirit" tree by drawing fruit and labeling each one with qualities like love, joy, and peace.

Week 3

Elijah

and the

Hidden

Treasure

The story of Elijah and his friends kept spreading, and their faith was inspiring people far and wide. One day, while hanging out at the park, they stumbled upon a mysterious, old map hidden under a loose brick near the tree they hang out at. It looked ancient, with faded lines and strange symbols. At the bottom, it read, "To those with faith, treasures untold await."

Elijah, eyes sparkling with excitement, said, "Y'all, this could be something big. What if this treasure helps even more people?"

The crew decided to follow the map. Their journey led them to an abandoned warehouse on the outskirts of the Rialto. The place was spooky, with creaking floors and cobwebs everywhere. As they ventured deeper, they stumbled upon a locked door with a riddle inscribed on it: "With faith, the path will clear; speak your prayer and have no fear."

Elijah gathered his friends, and they prayed together, asking for guidance and courage. As they finished, the door slowly creaked open, revealing a hidden room filled with chests and ancient artifacts.

Among the treasures, they found a golden key with another note: "Use this key with faith, and you'll unlock even greater rewards."

Their adventure didn't stop there. The key led them to various places around the city—a church, a library, and even a children's hospital. At each location, they discovered ways to help others, whether it was volunteering, donating, or simply spreading hope through their story and prayers. The real treasure, they realized, was the impact they were making on people's lives.

One day, while at the children's hospital, they met a boy named Carlos who had been in a wheelchair for years. His dream was to walk again, but doctors had said it was impossible. Inspired by Elijah's unwavering faith, Carlos started to pray, and Elijah and his friends joined him every day, believing in a miracle.

Weeks passed, and one morning, Carlos felt a tingling in his legs. With a determined look, he stood up, taking his first steps in years. The hospital was in awe, and news of the miracle spread like wildfire. People were drawn to Carlos' story, finding new hope and belief in the power of prayer.

DAY 15

"Give all your worries to him, because he cares for you."
1 Peter 5:7 (ICB)

Prayer Prompt

Pray to give all your worries to God because He cares for you.

Activity

Write down or draw one thing that worries you, then crumple the paper and throw it away as a way to give your worries to God.

DAY 16

"Do not be shaped by this world. Instead, be changed within by a new way of thinking."
Romans 12:2 (ICB)

Prayer Prompt

Pray that God will help you think good thoughts and not follow the crowd.

Activity

Draw two pictures—one of what happens when you follow God's way and another when you follow the world.

New Way of Thinking
Day 16 Ho boltlal laisg foll o hoa God's way

Folllowing God's way

New Way of Thinking
Flolling God fellled roling ou folowing the woh

Folllowing the he wold

DAY 17

"You should be a light for other people. Live so that they will see the good things you do."

Matthew 5:16 (ICB)

Prayer Prompt

Ask God to help you shine your light so others can see how great He is.

Activity

Make a "shine bright" bracelet using beads or string as a reminder to let your light shine for God.

DAY 18

"So don't worry, because I am with you. Don't be afraid, because I am your God."

Isaiah 41:10 (ICB)

Prayer Prompt

Pray for courage when you are afraid, knowing God is always with you.

Activity

Make a "God's Got Me" shield using a piece of cardboard and decorate it to remind you God protects you.

DAY 19

"I can do all things through Christ because he gives me strength."

Philippians 4:13 (ICB)

Prayer Prompt

Ask God to help you do your best in everything.

Activity

Write down one thing you find hard to do and ask God to give you the strength to do it.

DAY 20

"If anyone belongs to Christ, then he is made new. The old things have gone; everything is made new!"

2 Corinthians 5:17 (ICB)

Prayer Prompt

Thank God for making you a new person when you follow Jesus.

Activity

Draw a before-and-after picture of something transforming (like a caterpillar to a butterfly) to remind you of how God transforms you.

DAY 21

"Enjoy serving the Lord. And he will give you what you want."

Psalm 37:4 (ICB)

Prayer Prompt

Ask God to help your heart want what He wants for you.

Activity

Cut out a heart from paper and write or draw things inside it that you know God wants for your life.

Closer frierndship with God.

Week 4

Elijah and the Faithful Journey

Elijah and his friends had discovered many treasures, both tangible and intangible, through their adventures. Their faith and prayers had brought them rain, healed the sick, and inspired countless people. But their journey was far from over.

One evening, while sitting around a cozy firepit, Mia brought out the old map again. "Guys, there's one more spot we haven't explored," she pointed out. "It's marked with a special symbol. What if it's our biggest adventure yet?"

Elijah nodded, "Let's do this. Tomorrow, we head out at dawn."

The next morning, they set off, following the map to a dense forest on the outskirts of the city. The path was rugged, and they had to navigate through thick bushes and climb over fallen trees. But their faith kept them going.

As they ventured deeper, they stumbled upon an ancient stone archway, covered in vines. An inscription read, "Only those with pure hearts and unshakable faith may enter."

Elijah took a deep breath and led the way. They stepped through the archway and found themselves in a hidden valley, filled with vibrant flowers and crystal-clear streams. In the center of the valley stood an enormous tree, its branches reaching toward the sky.

At the base of the tree was a small, wooden box with intricate carvings. Elijah opened it and found a collection of scrolls. Each scroll contained powerful prayers and stories of miracles from people all around the world. There was also a letter that read, "To those who find this, continue to spread the power of prayer and faith. Use these prayers to bring hope and change."

Elijah and his friends knew they had found something extraordinary. They read the scrolls and felt a deep connection to the people who had written them. Their faith was stronger than ever.

They decided to take the scrolls back to the city and share them with everyone. They organized community prayer meetings, where people from all walks of life came together to pray and share their stories. The valley's message of hope and faith spread far and wide, inspiring even more miracles and acts of kindness.

Elijah realized that their journey wasn't just about finding treasure—it was about creating a community of faith and support. They had become a beacon of hope for everyone around the world.

DAY 22

"Come near to God, and God will come near to you."

James 4:8 (ICB)

Prayer Prompt

Pray for a closer friendship with God.

Activity

Write a letter to God as if you were writing to a friend.

DAY 23

"Trust the Lord with all your heart. Don't depend on your own understanding. Remember the Lord in everything you do. And he will give you success."

Proverbs 3:5-6 (ICB)

Prayer Prompt

Pray that you will follow God's directions, not your own.

Activity

Make a map of your week and include time to pray and listen to God.

DAY 24

"With God's power working in us, he can do much, much more than anything we can ask or think of."

Ephesians 3:20 (ICB)

Prayer Prompt

Ask God to do amazing things in your life that are bigger than you can imagine.

Activity

Make a "dream jar" and write down one big thing you'd love God to do for you, then pray about it.

DAY 25

"Where God's love is, there is no fear. God's perfect love takes away fear."

1 John 4:18 (ICB)

Prayer Prompt

Pray for God's love to fill your heart so that you are not afraid.

Activity

Draw a big heart and write "God's love" inside it. Then write or draw all the ways you can share that love.

DAY 26

"Those who go to God Most High for safety will be protected."

Psalm 91:1 (ICB)

Prayer Prompt

Ask God to keep you safe and give you peace.

Activity

Build a fort or tent in your room and pretend it's a safe place, just like being in God's presence.

DAY 27

"Faith means being sure of the things we hope for. And faith means knowing that something is real even if we do not see it."

Hebrews 11:1 (ICB)

Prayer Prompt

Pray for faith to believe in God, even when you can't see what He's doing.

Activity

Play a game of "hide and seek," and remember that even when you can't see something, it's still there—just like God!

DAY 28

"Love is patient and kind. Love is not jealous, it does not brag, and it is not proud."

1 Corinthians 13:4 (ICB)

Prayer Prompt

Ask God to help you love others, even when it's hard.

Activity

Write or draw one way you can show love to someone this week.

ELIJAH AND THE POWER OF PERSISTENT PRAYER

Elijah and his friends had been through amazing adventures. From bringing rain to discovering hidden treasures, their faith and persistent prayers had moved mountains. But now, it was time for one final lesson—a lesson they wanted to share with all those who had been inspired by their journey.

Today, the community has come together, not just to celebrate the miracles they've seen, but to **welcome you as a new Junior Prayer Warrior**. Your journey through this 28-day prayer journal has been one of faith, discovery, and growth. And just as Elijah's prayers brought rain and healing, **so can yours.**

Remember, you too can pray like Elijah. With every prayer you've said, every moment of faith you've embraced, you've come closer to unlocking the power of persistent prayer. **You have the ability to move mountains, to bring hope and light to others through the power of your faith.**

This is just the beginning of your journey as a prayer warrior. **The same God who answered Elijah's prayers is listening to yours.** So, keep praying, keep believing, and keep trusting. You are now part of a community of believers who know that with prayer, anything is possible.

As we celebrate today, know that you are ready for what comes next. You've learned that faith, combined with persistent prayer, can change the world. And now, as you stand alongside Elijah and his friends in spirit, may you continue to walk in faith, lifting your prayers up to our God, the One who hears and answers.

Welcome, Junior Prayer Warrior! The adventure of faith continues, and your prayers will make a difference in the world. Keep praying and watch as God works wonders through you!

THE END! FOR NOW...

I hope this book was a blessing to you, as well as an enjoyable experience. Please consider purchasing copies of this for someone who can be inspired to

Pray Like Elijah.

God Bless you,

MARCUS BEARD